With oval looms designed for light and medium weight yarns, it's never been easier to knit a variety of projects for gifts and home décor. You'll love this collection!

3

12

21

LEISURE ARTS, INC. • Maumelle, Arkansas

Meet KATHY NORRIS

Like most people, Kathy Norris learned to knit in the traditional style, using knitting needles. She discovered loom knitting at the craft supply store where she worked in Southern California. She says, "They handed me a knitting loom and told me to figure it out. So I taught myself how to use it."

Kathy used her first loom knitting designs to teach others the fun new skill. In 2005, she began publishing her patterns. "I was attracted to loom knitting because, as a designer, you have to find a new way to work with the geometry of knitting. Once you have the loom knitting basics down, you can start experimenting to make the loom do what you want."

Look for Kathy's *Loom Knit Stitch Dictionary* (#75566) for easy and exciting pattern stitches to knit with looms of all sizes and shapes, including oval looms. Leisure Arts books and ebooks featuring Kathy's designs for looms using medium and bulky weight yarns are *More Knitting Wheel Fashions* (#4411), *I Can't Believe I'm Loom Knitting* (#5250), *Big Book of Loom Knitting* (#5604), *Loom Knitting for Mommy and Me* (#5942), *Loom Knit Dishcloths* (#6369), *Big Book of Loom Knit Cowls* (#6611), *Loom Knit Hats and Scarves* (#75471), and *Loom Knit Baby Wraps* (#6667). For more about Kathy, visit KathyNorrisDesigns.com.

#6369

#6611

#5942

#75566

HEART BABY BIB

(Instructions begin on page 4)

Heart
BABY BIB

EASY +

Finished Size: 7¼" wide x 6" high (18.5 cm x 15 cm)

SHOPPING LIST

Yarn (Light Weight) LIGHT 3

[1.75 ounces, 137 yards (50 grams, 125 meters) per skein]:

☐ 1 skein

Loom (oval, regular gauge)

☐ 54 Pegs

Additional Supplies

☐ Knitting loom tool

☐ Crochet hook, size H (5 mm)

GAUGE INFORMATION

In Garter Stitch (knit one row, purl one row),

20 stitches and 36 rows = 4" (10 cm)

STITCH GUIDE

CHAIN INCREASE

Place loop from last peg onto crochet hook and chain cast on 1 peg, place loop from hook on next empty peg.

LEFT DECREASE (uses 2 pegs)

Use the tool to move the loop from peg A to the **left** and place it on peg B. Knit peg B, lifting the bottom 2 loops over the working yarn and off the peg *(Figs. 6a & b, page 30)*.

FOLLOWING A CHART

The chart shows each stitch as a square. The white squares are knit stitches and the peach squares are purl stitches. Begin at the bottom edge of the chart. For ease in following the chart, place a ruler on the chart **above** the row being worked to help you keep your place.

BODY

Working on the **inside** of the loom from **right** to **left**, chain cast on 30 pegs *(Figs. 2a & b, page 27)*; work as flat knitting.

Row 1: Purl across, chain increase working on the **outside** of the loom *(Fig. 2c, page 28)*: 31 pegs used.

Row 2: Knit across, chain increase working on the **inside** of the loom: 32 pegs.

Rows 3-6: Repeat Rows 1 and 2 twice: 36 pegs used.

Row 7: Purl across.

Row 8: Knit across.

Row 9: P5, knit across to last 5 pegs, P5.

Row 10: Knit across.

Rows 11-47: Follow Chart.

Row 48: Knit across.

Row 49: Purl across.

Rows 50-53: Repeat Rows 48 and 49 twice.

Row 54: Left decrease, move loop to empty peg, knit across to last 2 pegs, left decrease: 34 pegs remaining.

Row 55: K4, work simple bind off across to last 4 pegs *(Figs. 7a & b, page 30)*, K4.

TIE

Work 4 stitch I-cord as follows:

★ Bring the working yarn across the inside of the loom, then outside to the **right** of the first peg of the 4-peg group *(Fig. A)*. Working from **right** to **left**, knit the 4 pegs; repeat from ★ until cord measures approximately 11½" (29 cm), giving the cord a tug every few rows to close the gap between the first and last stitches *(Fig. B)*.

Work simple bind off.

Fig. A

Fig. B

Beginning at the **right** of the remaining 4 pegs, K4.

Work 4-stitch I-cord for second Tie.

The bib may be blocked to give more definition to the heart.

CHART

KEY ☐ - knit ■ - purl

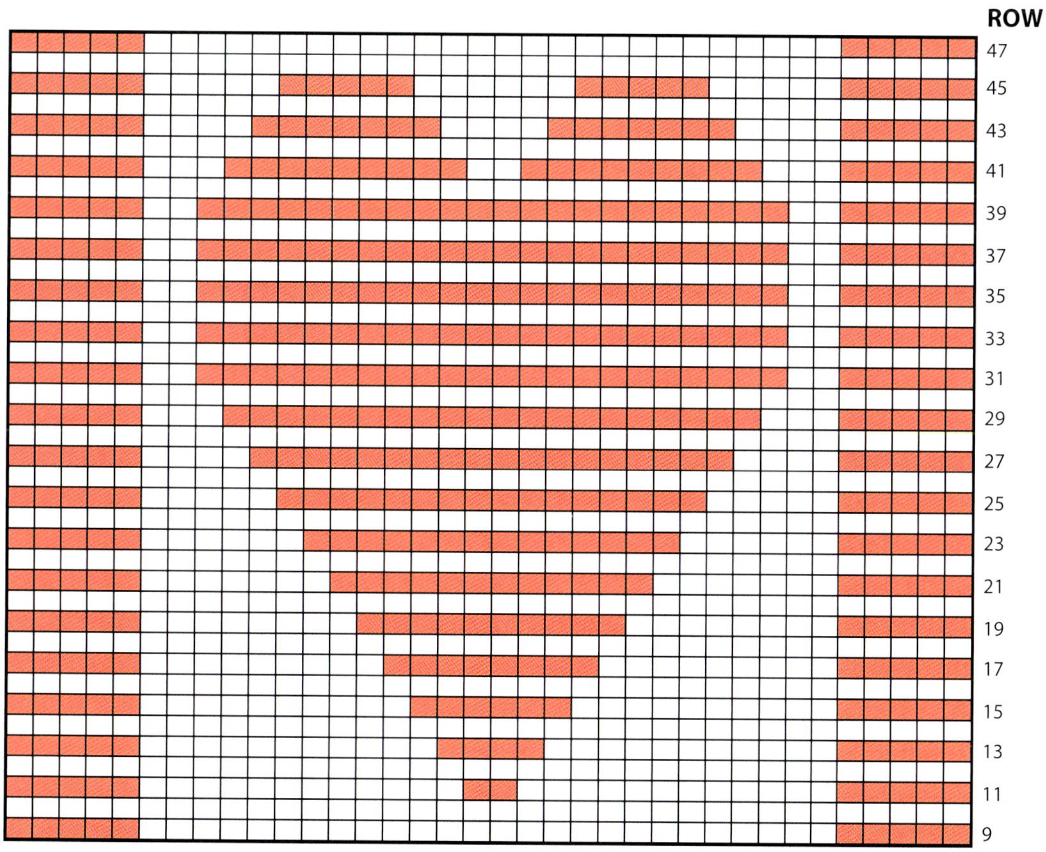

GARTER BOOTIES

EASY

Finished Size: 3½" long (9 cm)

SHOPPING LIST

Yarn (Light Weight) LIGHT 3

☐ 70 yards (64 meters)

Loom (oval, regular gauge)

☐ 54 Pegs

Additional Supplies

☐ Knitting loom tool

☐ Tapestry needle

☐ 5/8" (16 mm) Ribbon - 1 yard (1 meter)

GAUGE INFORMATION

In Garter Stitch (knit one row, purl one row),

20 stitches and 36 rows = 4" (10 cm)

STITCH GUIDE

LEFT DECREASE (uses 2 pegs)

Use the tool to move the loop from peg A to the **left** and place it on peg B. Knit peg B, lifting the bottom 2 loops over the working yarn and off the peg ***(Figs. 6a & b, page 30)***.

Garter BOOTIES

BODY

Working from **left** to **right**, e-wrap cast on 36 pegs ***(Figs. 1a-e, page 27)***; work as flat knitting.

Row 1: Knit across.

Row 2: Purl across.

Rows 3-16: Repeat Rows 1 and 2, 7 times.

SHAPING

Row 1 (Decrease row)**:** K1, left decrease, knit across to last 3 pegs, left decrease, K1: 34 pegs remaining.

As each decrease is formed, move the loop from the edge peg closest to the loops on the same side of the loom.

Row 2: Purl across.

Rows 3-6: Repeat Rows 1 and 2 twice: 30 pegs remaining.

Row 7: Simple bind off 2 pegs ***(Figs. 7a & b, page 30)***, knit across: 28 pegs remaining.

Row 8: Simple bind off 2 pegs, purl across: 26 pegs remaining.

CUFF

Row 1 (Eyelet row)**:** K1, ★ left decrease, move loop just made to empty peg, e-wrap empty peg counterclockwise; repeat from ★ across to last peg, K1.

Row 2: Purl across.

Row 3: Knit across.

Rows 4-11: Repeat Rows 2 and 3, 4 times.

Bind off using sewn bind off ***(Figs. 10a & b, page 31)***; do **not** cut yarn.

Fold Bootie in half. Beginning at Cuff edge, weave end of rows together ***(Fig. 11, page 31)***, then sew across cast on stitches.

Beginning at front, weave an 18" (45.5 cm) length of ribbon through eyelet row; tie in a bow.

LACY STRIPES BABY BLANKET

INTERMEDIATE

Finished Size: 27½" x 32" (70 cm x 81.5 cm)

SHOPPING LIST

Yarn (Light Weight) LIGHT 3

[3.5 ounces, 394 yards (100 grams, 360 meters) per skein]:

- ☐ 3 skeins

Loom (oval, regular gauge)

- ☐ 70 Pegs

Additional Supplies

- ☐ Knitting loom tool
- ☐ Crochet hook, size H (5 mm)
- ☐ Tapestry needle

GAUGE INFORMATION

In Garter Stitch (knit one row, purl one row),
20 stitches and 36 rows = 4" (10 cm)
Right Panel = 14" (35.5 cm) wide

Lacy Stripes BABY BLANKET

STITCH GUIDE

YRP, DECREASE, YRP (uses 3 pegs)

Skip next peg, use the tool to move the loop from next peg (peg A) to the peg on the **left** (peg B) ***(Fig. A)***. Move loop from skipped peg to empty peg (peg A). E-wrap the empty peg counterclockwise to create the YRP (yarn around peg). With yarn at inside of loom, skip next peg (peg A). Knit peg B, lifting the bottom 2 loops over the working yarn and off the peg ***(Fig. B)***. Move the loop from skipped peg to peg B. Lift the bottom loop over the top loop and off the peg without knitting it. Move loop to empty peg, YRP.

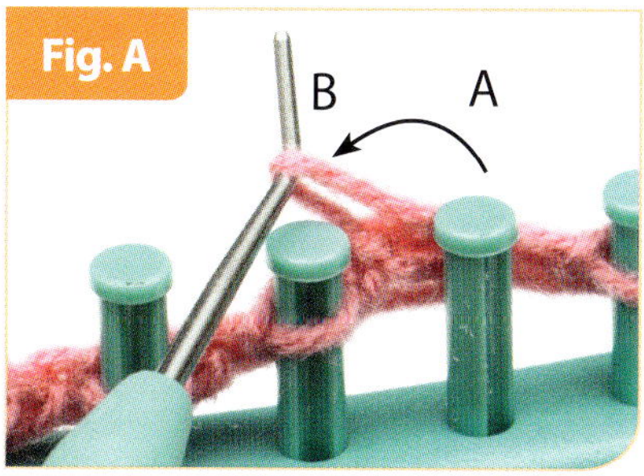

Fig. A

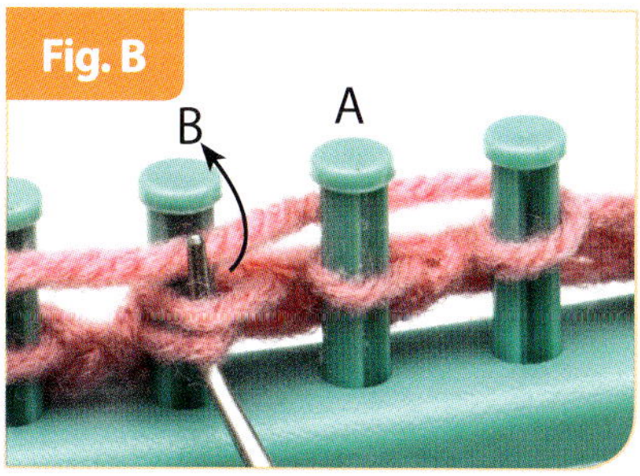

Fig. B

RIGHT PANEL

BOTTOM BORDER

Working on the **inside** of the loom from **right** to **left**, chain cast on all 70 pegs ***(Figs. 2a & b, page 27)***; work as flat knitting.

Row 1: Knit across.

Row 2: Purl across.

Rows 3-6: Repeat Rows 1 and 2 twice.

BODY

Four pegs on the right edge of the Panel form the side border.

Row 1: K5, P3, (K1, P3) across to last 2 pegs, K2.

Row 2: Knit across to last 4 pegs, P4.

Rows 3 and 4: Repeat Rows 1 and 2.

Row 5: K5, YRP, decrease, YRP, ★ K1, YRP, decrease, YRP; repeat from ★ across to last 2 pegs, K2.

Row 6: Knit across to last 4 pegs, P4.

Repeat Rows 1-6 for pattern until Panel measures approximately 31½" (80 cm) from cast on edge, ending by working Row 6.

TOP BORDER

Row 1: Knit across.

Row 2: Purl across.

Rows 3-6: Repeat Rows 1 and 2 twice.

Work double wrap bind off across leaving a long end for sewing ***(Figs. 8a & b, page 30)***.

LEFT PANEL

BOTTOM BORDER

Working on the **inside** of the loom from **right** to **left**, chain cast on 69 pegs; work as flat knitting.

Row 1: Knit across.

Row 2: Purl across.

Rows 3-6: Repeat Rows 1 and 2 twice.

BODY

Four pegs on the left edge of the Panel form the side border.

Row 1: (K1, P3) across to last 5 pegs, K5.

Row 2: P4, knit across.

Rows 3 and 4: Repeat Rows 1 and 2.

Row 5: ★ K1, YRP, decrease, YRP; repeat from ★ across to last 5 pegs, K5.

Row 6: P4, knit across.

Repeat Rows 1-6 for pattern until Left Panel measures same as Right Panel, ending by working Row 6.

TOP BORDER

Row 1: Knit across.

Row 2: Purl across.

Rows 3-6: Repeat Rows 1 and 2 twice.

Work double wrap bind off across.

Weave long edge of Panels together ***(Fig. 11, page 31)***, placing side borders at outer edges and being careful to match pattern rows.

Baby will be cute and lovable in this heart-decorated bib! Matching socks will keep baby's feet warm, and the ribbon accent makes sure they stay on. A colorful afghan provides a soft place to play and snuggle up!

GARTER CHECKS COWL

BEGINNER

Finished Size:
24½" circumference x
7¼" high (62 cm x 18.5 cm)

SHOPPING LIST

Yarn (Medium Weight) MEDIUM 4
[5 ounces, 230 yards
(141 grams, 211 meters) per skein]:
- ☐ 1 skein

Loom (oval, regular gauge)
- ☐ 70 Pegs

Additional Supplies
- ☐ Knitting loom tool
- ☐ Crochet hook, size H (5 mm)

GAUGE INFORMATION

In Twisted Garter Stitch (e-wrap knit one rnd, purl one rnd),
10 stitches and 20 rnds/rows = 3½" (9 cm)

Garter CHECKS COWL

BODY

Working on the **inside** of the loom from **right** to **left**, chain cast on all 70 pegs ***(Figs. 2a & b, page 27)***; work as circular knitting.

Rnd 1: E-wrap knit around.

Rnd 2: (P5, EWK5) around.

Rnds 3-6: Repeat Rnds 1 and 2 twice.

Rnd 7: (EWK5, P5) around.

Rnd 8: E-wrap knit around.

Rnds 9-11: Repeat Rnds 7 and 8 once, then repeat Rnd 7 once **more**.

Rnd 12: (P5, EWK5) around.

Rnd 13: E-wrap knit around.

Rnds 14-16: Repeat Rnds 12 and 13 once, then repeat Rnd 12 once **more**.

Rnds 17-42: Repeat Rnds 7-16 twice, then repeat Rnds 7 and 8, 3 times.

Work double wrap bind off around ***(Figs. 8a & b, page 30)***.

BUTTON-UP GAUNTLETS

Button-Up GAUNTLETS

INTERMEDIATE

Finished Size: 7" palm x 13" long (18 cm x 33 cm)

SHOPPING LIST

Yarn (Medium Weight) 4
[4 ounces, 200 yards (113 grams, 183 meters) per skein]:
- ☐ 1 skein

Loom (oval, regular gauge)
- ☐ 70 Pegs

Additional Supplies
- ☐ Knitting loom tool
- ☐ Crochet hook, size H (5 mm)
- ☐ Yarn needle
- ☐ Sewing needle and matching thread
- ☐ ½" (12 mm) Buttons - 14

GAUGE INFORMATION

In Stockinette Stitch (knit each row), 16 stitches and 20 rows = 4" (10 cm)

STITCH GUIDE

LEFT DECREASE (uses 2 pegs)
Use the tool to move the loop from peg A to the **left** and place it on peg B. Knit peg B, lifting the bottom 2 loops over the working yarn and off the peg ***(Figs. 6a & b, page 30)***.

YRP, LEFT DECREASE (uses 2 pegs)
A hole is made to form a buttonhole.

Worked from left to right:
Use the tool to move the loop from peg A to the **left** and place it on peg B ***(Fig. 6a, page 30)***. Move both loops to empty peg, e-wrap empty peg clockwise to create YRP (yarn around peg). Knit peg A, lifting the bottom 2 loops over the working yarn and off the peg ***(Fig. 6b, page 30)***.

Worked from right to left:
Use the tool to move the loop from peg A to the **left** and place it on peg B. E-wrap empty peg counterclockwise. Knit peg B, lifting the bottom 2 loops over the working yarn and off the peg.

LEFT MITT

RIBBING

Working on the **inside** of the loom from **right** to **left**, chain cast on 44 pegs ***(Figs. 2a & b, page 27)***; work as flat knitting.

Row 1: K9, P1, (K1, P1) across to last 4 pegs, K4.

Row 2: K4, P1, (K1, P1) across to last 9 pegs, K9.

Row 3: K9, P1, (K1, P1) across to last 4 pegs, K4.

Row 4: K4, (P1, K1) across to last 8 pegs, left decrease, K6: 43 pegs remaining.

As each decrease is formed, move the loops from the edge pegs closest to the loops on the same side of the loom.

Row 5: K8, P1, (K1, P1) across to last 4 pegs, K4.

Row 6: K1, YRP, left decrease (buttonhole made), (K1, P1) across to last 8 pegs, K8.

Row 7: K8, P1, (K1, P1) across to last 4 pegs, K4.

Row 8: K4, P1, (K1, P1) across to last 8 pegs, K8.

Rows 9-11: Repeat Rows 7 and 8 once, then repeat Row 7 once **more**.

Row 12: K1, YRP, left decrease, (K1, P1) across to last 8 pegs, K8.

Row 13: K8, P1, (K1, P1) across to last 4 pegs, K4.

Row 14: K4, (P1, K1) across to last 7 pegs, left decrease, K5: 42 pegs remaining.

Row 15: K7, P1, (K1, P1) across to last 4 pegs, K4.

Row 16: K4, P1, (K1, P1) across to last 7 pegs, K7.

Row 17: K7, P1, (K1, P1) across to last 4 pegs, K4.

Row 18: K1, YRP, left decrease, (K1, P1) across to last 7 pegs, K7.

Rows 19-23: Repeat Rows 15 and 16 twice, then repeat Row 15 once **more**.

Row 24: K1, YRP, left decrease, K1, (P1, K1) across to last 6 pegs, left decrease, K4: 41 pegs remaining.

Row 25: K6, P1, (K1, P1) across to last 4 pegs, K4.

Row 26: K4, P1, (K1, P1) across to last 6 pegs, K6.

Rows 27-29: Repeat Rows 25 and 26 once, then repeat Row 25 once **more**.

Row 30: K1, YRP, left decrease, (K1, P1) across to last 6 pegs, K6.

Rows 31-35: Repeat Rows 25 and 26 twice, then repeat Row 25 once **more**.

Row 36: K1, YRP, left decrease, K1, (P1, K1) across to last 5 pegs, left decrease, K3: 40 pegs remaining.

Row 37: K5, P1, (K1, P1) across to last 4 pegs, K4.

Row 38: K4, P1, (K1, P1) across to last 5 pegs, K5.

Rows 39-41: Repeat Rows 37 and 38 once, then repeat Row 37 once **more**.

Row 42: K1, YRP, left decrease, (K1, P1) across to last 5 pegs, K5.

HAND

Rows 1-14: Knit across.

Row 15: K 25, leave remaining 15 pegs unworked.

THUMB

Row 1: K 10, leave remaining 15 pegs unworked.

Rows 2-6: K 10.

Work chain one bind off across the 10 pegs *(**Figs. 9a-c, page 31**)*.

PALM

Work across 15 pegs on one side of Thumb for first side.

Rows 1-7: Knit across.

Rows 8-12: K1, (P1, K1) across.

Work chain one bind off across leaving a long end for sewing.

Repeat on remaining set of 15 pegs for second side.

Fold Mitt in half. Using long end at top outer edge of Mitt, weave end of rows together to the Ribbing *(**Fig. 11, page 31**)*.

Using long end at top inner edge of Mitt, weave end of rows together to top of the Thumb.

Sew buttons to Mitt corresponding with buttonholes.

RIGHT MITT

RIBBING

Working on the **outside** of the loom from **right** to **left**, chain cast on 44 pegs *(**Fig. 2c, page 28**)*; work as flat knitting.

Complete same as Left Mitt.

CHECKS HAT

(Instructions begin on page 18)

EASY +

FINISHED SIZE

Child: 13½" (34.5 cm) circumference

Adult: 17½" (44.5 cm) circumference

Size Note: We have printed the instructions for the sizes in different colors to make it easier for you to find:
- Child size in Blue
- Adult size in Pink

Instructions in Black apply to all sizes.

SHOPPING LIST

Yarn (Medium Weight) 4

[4 ounces, 200 yards (113 grams, 183 meters) per skein]:
- ☐ Color A (Green) - 1 skein

[5 ounces, 251 yards (142 grams, 230 meters) per skein]:
- ☐ Color B (Yellow) - 1 skein

Loom (oval, regular gauge)
- ☐ Child - 54 Pegs
- ☐ Adult - 70 Pegs

Additional Supplies
- ☐ Knitting loom tool
- ☐ Crochet hook, size H (5 mm)
- ☐ Yarn needle

GAUGE INFORMATION

In Stockinette Stitch color pattern (knit each rnd),
16 stitches and 32 rnds/rows = 4" (10 cm)

Checks HAT

STITCH GUIDE

RIGHT DECREASE (uses 2 pegs)

Use the tool to move the loop from peg B to the **right** and place it on peg A ***(Fig. A)***. Knit peg A, lifting the bottom 2 loops over the working yarn and off the peg ***(Fig. B)***.

Fig. A

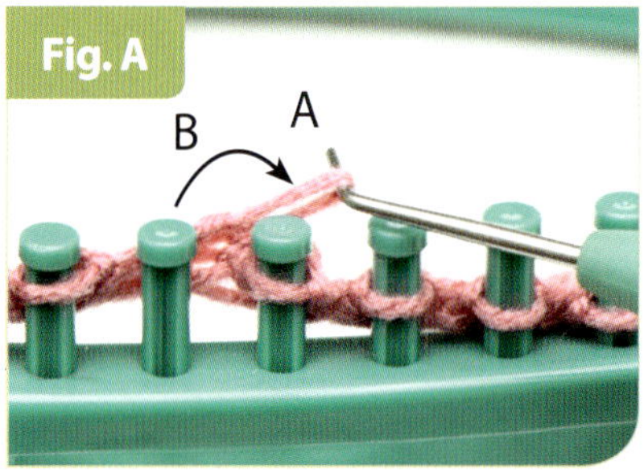

Fig. B

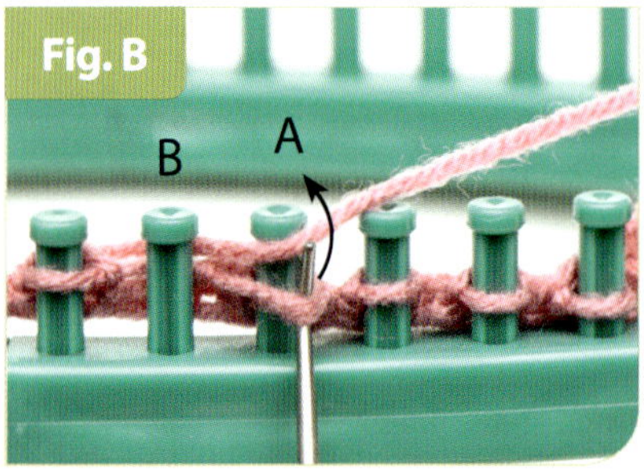

RIBBING

Working on the **inside** of the loom from **right** to **left** and using Color A, chain cast on all 54{70} pegs ***(Figs. 2a & b, page 27)***; work as circular knitting.

At the end of Rnd 1, drop Color A to the inside of the loom and begin working with Color B leaving a long end to weave in later; do **not** cut yarn. Always place unused yarn at the inside of the loom.

Rnd 1: With Color A, (K1, P1) around.

Rnd 2: With Color B, (K1, P1) around.

Rnds 3-10: Repeat Rnds 1 and 2, 4 times.

BODY

When instructed to skip 1, bring the yarn to the inside of the loom behind the peg to be skipped *(Fig. C)*, then back to the outside ready to knit the next peg.

Fig. C

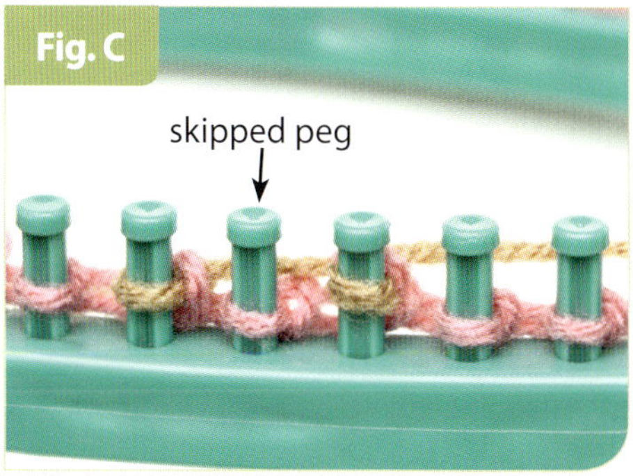

Rnd 1: With Color A, knit around.

Rnd 2: With Color B, (skip 1, K1) around.

Rnd 3: With Color A, knit around.

Rnd 4: With Color B, (K1, skip 1) around.

Rnds 5 thru 59{63}: Repeat Rnds 1-4, 13{14} times; then repeat Rnds 1-3 once **more**.

Cut Color A.

Rnd 60{64}: With Color B, work right decrease around: 27{35} pegs remaining.

GATHERED REMOVAL

Cut Color B leaving a long end for sewing. Thread the yarn needle with the yarn end. Beginning with the first peg, insert the yarn needle in the loop from **bottom** to **top** *(Fig. D)* and lift it off the peg, sliding it onto the yarn end. Repeat for each loop around the loom.

Fig. D

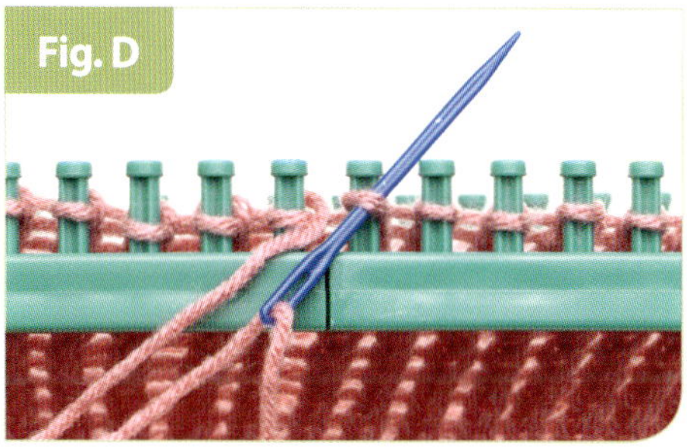

With the yarn end to the **wrong** side of the hat, pull the end **tightly**, gathering the loops to the center *(Fig. E)*; knot the yarn tightly and weave in the end; clip end close to work.

Fig. E

Stay fashion forward with this knit combination! Fingerless gauntlets provide a pop of color with contrasting buttons while keeping fingers free. The cowl keeps the neck warm without bulk, and the matching hat adds a stylish finishing touch!

Make your home inviting and cozy! This pillow provides a perfect lounging buddy, and the afghan keeps loved ones comfy and warm. Made in coordinating colors, these accents are sure to add style to any room!

LEISURE TIME PILLOW

BEGINNER

Finished Size: 16" (40.5 cm) square

SHOPPING LIST

Yarn (Medium Weight) 4
[3 ounces, 197 yards
(85 grams, 180 meters) per skein]:
- ☐ 2 skeins

Loom (oval, regular gauge)
- ☐ 54 Pegs

Additional Supplies
- ☐ Knitting loom tool
- ☐ Yarn needle
- ☐ 16" (40.5 cm) Pillow form

GAUGE INFORMATION

In pattern,
12 stitches = 4" (10 cm),
24 rows = 5" (12.75 cm)

Leisure Time PILLOW

BODY

Working from **left** to **right**, e-wrap cast on 50 pegs *(Figs. 1a-e, page 27)*; work as flat knitting.

Rows 1-5: E-wrap knit across.

Rows 6-10: EWK2, (P1, EWK1) across.

Rows 11-190: Repeat Rows 1-10, 18 times.

Rows 191 and 192: E-wrap knit across.

Work double wrap bind off across *(Figs. 8a & b, page 30)*.

Fold Body in half with **wrong** sides together. Weave end of rows together *(Fig. 11, page 31)* and sew cast on and bound off edge together, inserting pillow form before closing.

LEISURE TIME LAP ROBE

BEGINNER

Finished Size: 34¾" x 37" (88.5 cm x 94 cm)

SHOPPING LIST

Yarn (Medium Weight) MEDIUM 4

[3.5 ounces, 151 yards (100 grams, 138 meters) per skein]:

- ☐ 5 skeins

Loom (oval, regular gauge)

- ☐ 70 Pegs

Additional Supplies

- ☐ Knitting loom tool
- ☐ Crochet hook, size H (5 mm)
- ☐ Yarn needle

GAUGE INFORMATION

In pattern (Left and Right Panels), 12 stitches = 4" (10 cm), 24 rows = 5" (12.75 cm)

Leisure Time LAP ROBE

LEFT PANEL

Working on the **inside** of the loom from **right** to **left**, chain cast on 26 pegs ***(Figs. 2a & b, page 27)***; work as flat knitting.

Four pegs on the edge of the Panel form the side border.

Rows 1-3: (EWK1, P1) across to last 2 pegs, EWK2.

Row 4: (EWK1, P1) twice, e-wrap knit across.

Row 5: E-wrap knit across to last 3 pegs, P1, EWK2.

Rows 6-8: Repeat Rows 4 and 5 once, then repeat Row 4 once **more**.

Repeat Rows 1-8 for pattern until Panel measures 37" (94 cm) from cast on edge, ending by working Row 3.

Work chain one bind off across ***(Figs. 9a-c, page 31)***.

RIGHT PANEL

Working on the **outside** of the loom from **right** to **left**, chain cast on 26 pegs ***(Fig. 2c, page 28)***; work as flat knitting.

Work same as Left Panel.

CENTER PANEL

Working on the **inside** of the loom from **right** to **left**, chain cast on 56 pegs; work as flat knitting.

Row 1: E-wrap knit across.

Row 2: EWK3, P2, (EWK2, P2) across to last 3 pegs, EWK3.

Repeat Rows 1 and 2 for pattern until Panel measures same as Left Panel, ending by working Row 1.

Work chain one bind off across.

Weave long edges of Left and Right Panels to Center Panel, placing side borders at outer edges ***(Fig. 11, page 31)***.

General INSTRUCTIONS

ABBREVIATIONS

cm	centimeters
EWK	e-wrap knit
K	knit
mm	millimeters
P	purl
Rnd(s)	Round(s)
YRP	yarn around peg

SYMBOLS & TERMS

★ — work instructions following ★ as many **more** times as indicated in addition to the first time.

( ) or **[ ]** — work enclosed instructions **as many** times as specified by the number immediately following **or** contains explanatory remarks.

colon (:) — the number(s) given after a colon at the end of a row or round denote(s) the number of of pegs you should have occupied at the end of that row or round.

working yarn — the strand coming from the skein.

Yarn Weight Symbol & Names	LACE 0	SUPER FINE 1	FINE 2	LIGHT 3	MEDIUM 4	BULKY 5	SUPER BULKY 6	JUMBO 7
Type of Yarns in Category	Fingering, size 10 crochet thread	Sock, Fingering, Baby	Sport, Baby	DK, Light Worsted	Worsted, Afghan, Aran	Chunky, Craft, Rug	Super Bulky, Roving	Jumbo, Roving

BEGINNER	Projects for first-time loom knitters using basic knit and purl stitches, and simple color changes.
EASY	Projects using basic stitches, repetitive stitch patterns, simple color changes, and simple shaping and finishing.
EASY +	Projects using basic stitches, repetitive stitch patterns, simple color changes, simple short rows, and simple shaping and finishing.
INTERMEDIATE	Projects with a variety of stitches, such as lace, also short rows, and mid-level shaping and finishing.

GAUGE

Gauge is the number of stitches and rows or rounds in every inch of your knitting and is used to control the finished size. Exact gauge is essential for proper size. Before beginning your project, make a sample swatch approximately 4" (10 cm) wide with the yarn and loom specified in the individual instructions. After completing the swatch, give it a tug, holding the cast on and bound off edges, then let it "rest". Measure it, counting your stitches and rows carefully. If your swatch is larger or smaller than specified, make another, changing your tension of the working yarn as you form the stitches. Keep trying until you find the tension you need to achieve gauge. Maintain established gauge throughout project.

E-WRAP CAST ON

Leaving a 12" (30.5 cm) end outside the loom, wrap the working yarn around any peg to begin (peg A) in a **clockwise** direction, ending at the inside of the loom and behind the next peg (peg B) ***(Fig. 1a, e-wrap made)***.

Fig. 1a

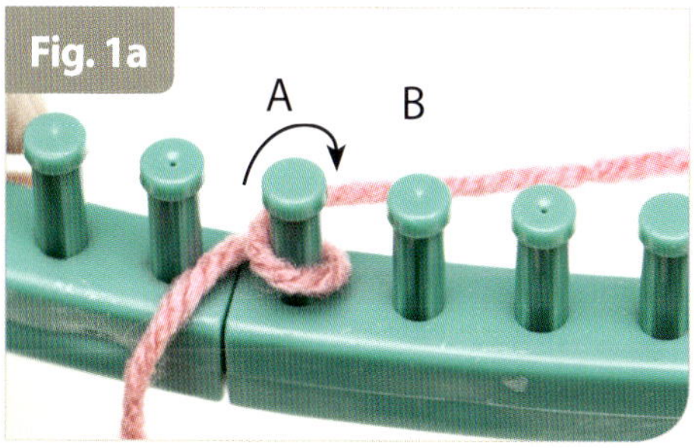

TIP

It is absolutely essential to wrap the working yarn loose enough to be able to later lift the loop off the peg, but not so loose that it falls off. As you wrap, let the yarn gently slide through your hand.

Moving around the loom **counterclockwise** (from left to right) and wrapping each peg with the same tension, e-wrap the next peg (peg B) **clockwise**, ending at the inside of the loom and behind the next peg ***(Fig. 1b)***.

Fig. 1b

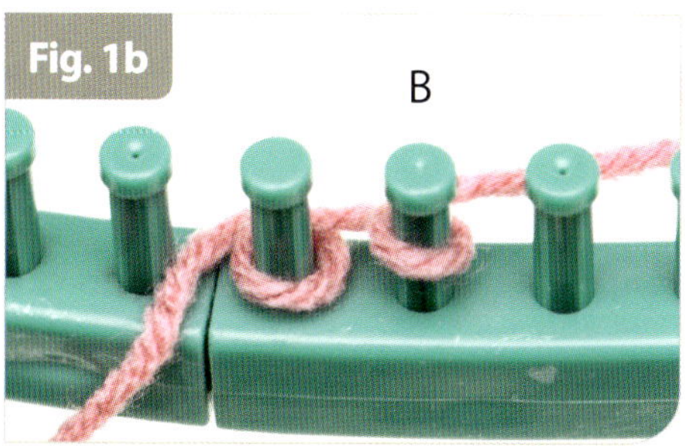

Continue around the loom, pushing the loops down with your other hand as you go, for as many pegs as specified for the project that you are making.

Fig. 1c

TIP

As you push the loops down, leave your finger on the last loop to prevent it from falling off.

The yarn should cross behind each peg at the inside edge of the loom ***(Fig. 1d)***, while leaving a loop on the outside of each peg ***(Fig. 1e)***.

Fig. 1d

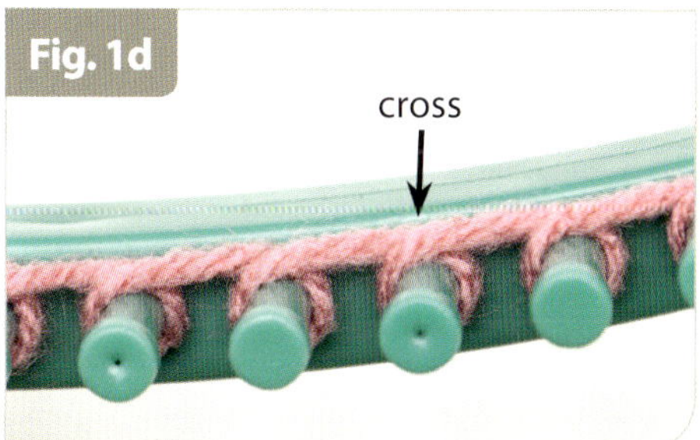

Fig. 1e

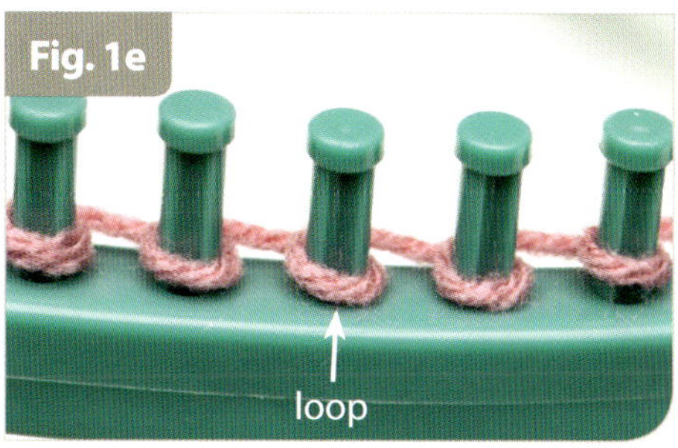

CHAIN CAST ON

Begin with a slip knot on your crochet hook. ★ Working on the **inside** of the loom, you will cast on from **right** to **left**. Wrap the working yarn around the outside of the peg and bring it to the inside. Lay the working yarn on top of the crochet hook with the peg being encircled by the yarn. Catching the working yarn with the hook, bring it through the loop on the hook ***(Fig. 2a)***, producing a chain stitch with the peg in the middle of the chain stitch.

Fig. 2a

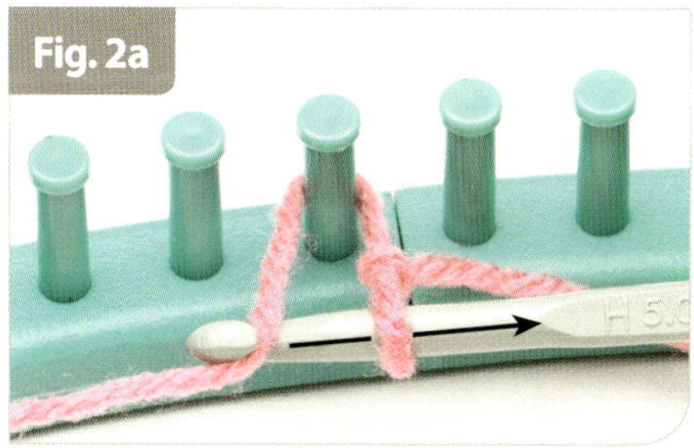

Repeat from ★ until you have cast on all but one peg needed.

For the last cast on stitch, keep the working yarn to the inside of the loom and place the loop from the hook onto the next empty peg ***(Fig. 2b)***. Turn the loom to work on the outside.

Fig. 2b

To chain cast on or chain increase working on the outside of the loom, hold the working yarn and crochet hook inside the loom. Work the same as before, only wrapping the yarn around the outside of the pegs *(Fig. 2c)*.

Fig. 2c

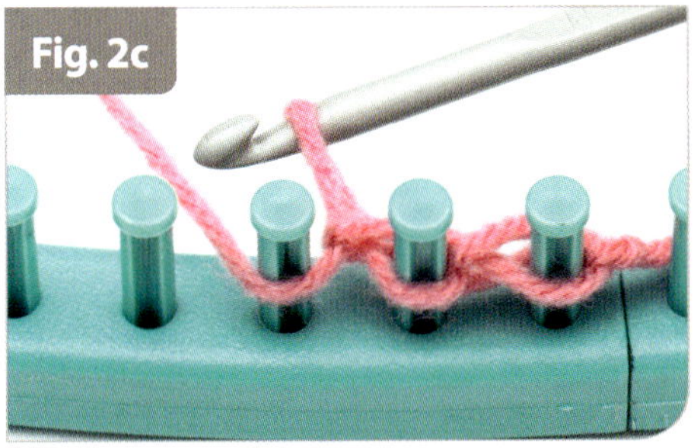

E-WRAP KNIT STITCH

(abbreviated EWK)

WORKING CIRCULARLY

When working **circularly** (making a tubular project), always work around the loom **counterclockwise** wrapping the pegs in the **same direction** as the e-wrap cast on.

Step 1: Wrap the next peg **clockwise** *(Fig. 3a)*. There will be 2 loops on the peg.

Fig. 3a

Step 2: Using the tool, lift the bottom loop over the top loop and off the peg *(Fig. 3b)*, completing the e-wrap knit stitch.

Fig. 3b

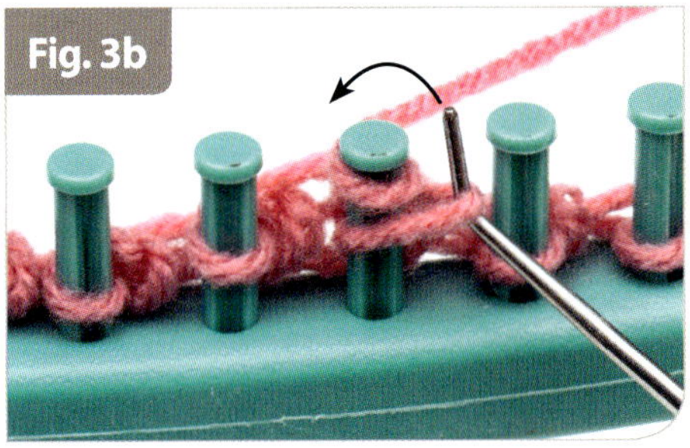

Repeat Steps 1 and 2 for each e-wrap knit stitch.

If all of the pegs in a round are to be e-wrapped knit, you can wrap all of the pegs at the same time (Step 1), then complete the stitches (Step 2) *(Fig. 3c)*.

Fig. 3c

WORKING FLAT

When working **flat** (back and forth in rows), the pegs are wrapped in the **opposite direction** on each row. The yarn should always cross at the inside edge of the loom while leaving a loop on the outside of each peg.

On a Left to Right Row

Work same as for Circular knitting *(Figs. 3a-c)*.

On a Right to Left Row

Step 1: Wrap the next peg **counterclockwise** *(Fig. 3d)*. There will be 2 loops on the peg.

Fig. 3d

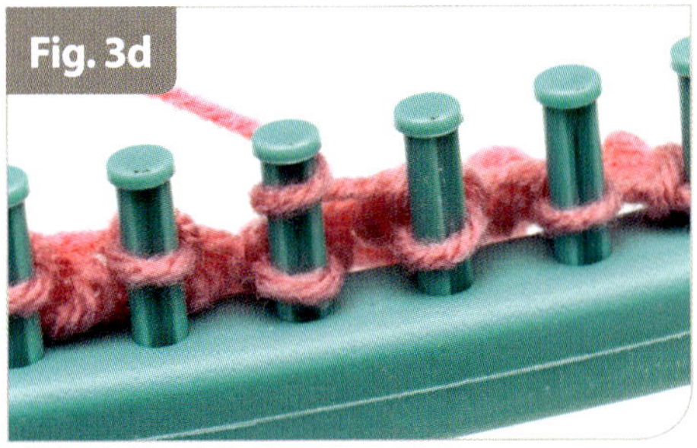

Step 2: Using the tool, lift the bottom loop over the top loop and off the peg *(Fig. 3e)*, completing the e-wrap knit stitch.

Fig. 3e

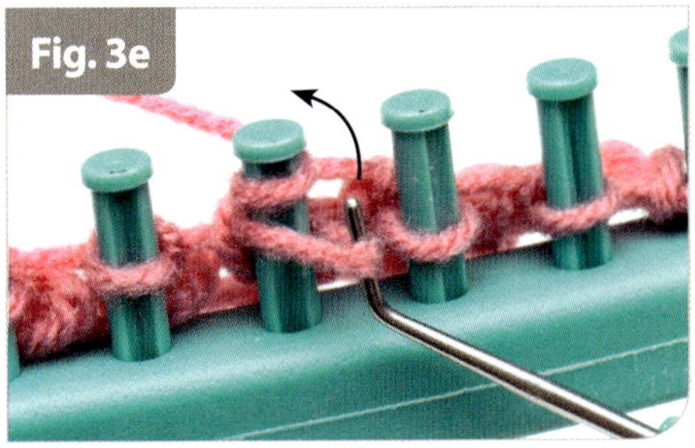

Repeat Steps 1 and 2 for each e-wrap knit stitch.

If the first peg of a row is e-wrap knit following the last peg of the previous row being e-wrap knit, the first peg is wrapped in the **same** direction as the last stitch on the previous row. The remaining pegs are wrapped in the **opposite** direction as the first peg.

KNIT STITCH *(abbreviated K)*

Step 1: Loosely lay the working yarn on the outside of the loom, **above** the loops that are already on the pegs ***(Fig. 4a)***.

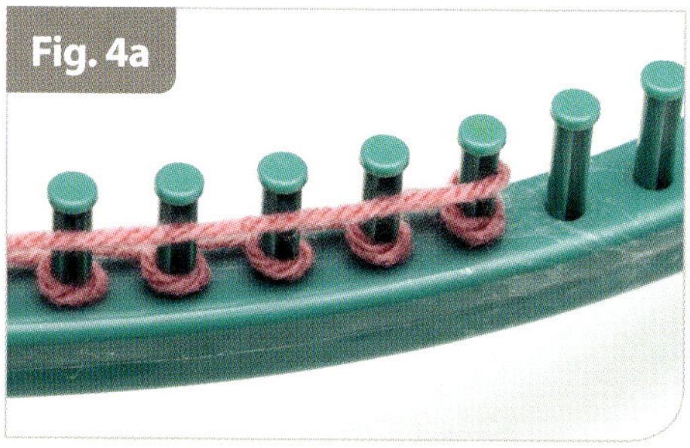

Fig. 4a

Step 2: Using the tool, lift the bottom loop over the working yarn and off the peg ***(Fig. 4b)***.

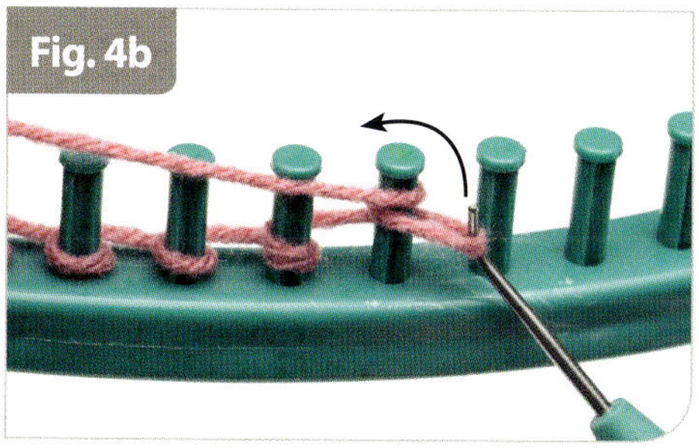

Fig. 4b

TIP

The working yarn should wrap around the peg as it forms a stitch ***(Fig. 4c)***. The stitches will form naturally if you gently push the back of the previous stitches down as you work.

Fig. 4c

PURL STITCH *(abbreviated P)*

Step 1: Lay the working yarn on the outside of the loom, **below** the loops on the pegs ***(Fig. 5a)***.

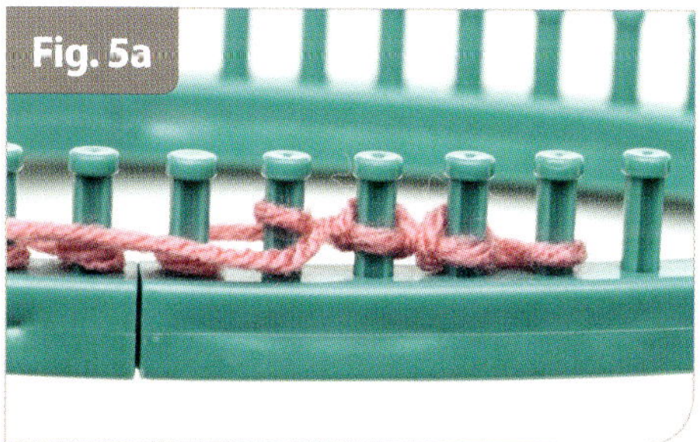

Fig. 5a

Step 2: Insert the tool down through the loop on the peg (from top to bottom) ***(Fig. 5b)***.

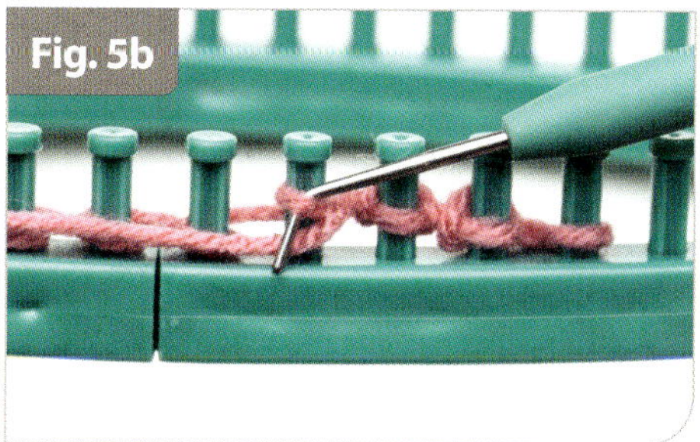

Fig. 5b

Step 3: With the tip of the tool over the working yarn, turn the tool as you pull the working yarn up through the loop on the peg forming a new loop ***(Fig. 5c)***.

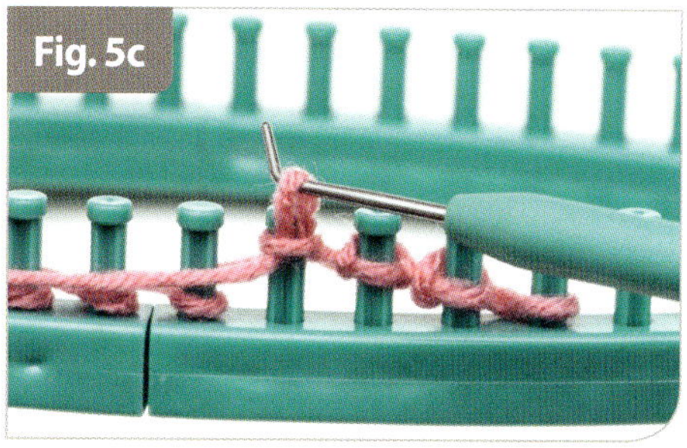

Fig. 5c

Step 4: Using your fingers, lift the original loop off the peg. Place the newly formed loop onto the empty peg ***(Fig. 5d)***. Tighten the loop by gently pulling the working yarn, allowing the stitch to curve around the outside half of the peg.

Fig. 5d

LEFT DECREASE

Use the tool to move the loop from peg A to the **left** and place it on peg B, leaving peg A empty ***(Fig. 6a)***. Knit peg B ***(Fig. 6b)***, lifting the bottom loops over the working yarn.

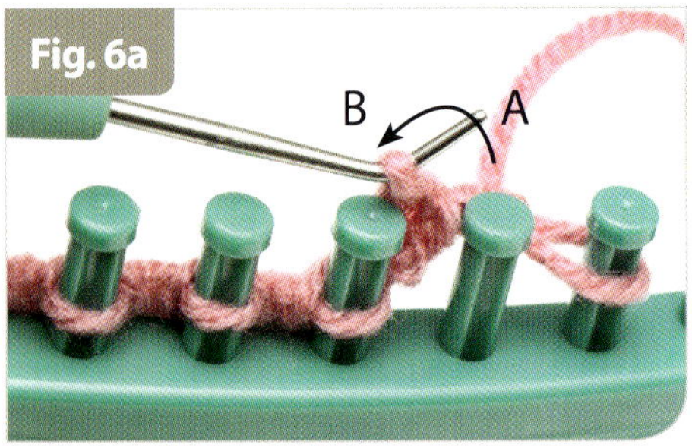

Fig. 6a

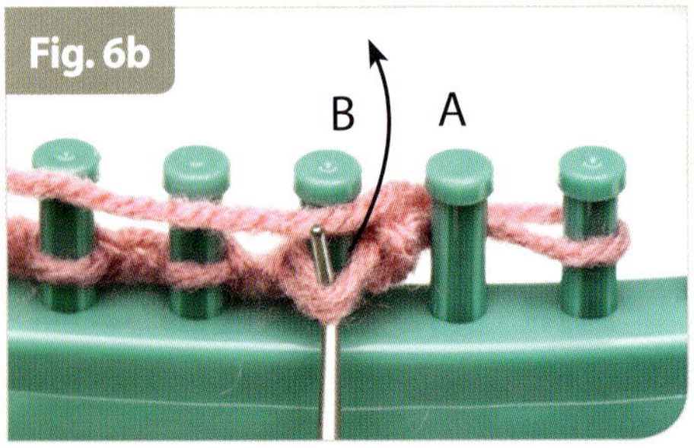

Fig. 6b

SIMPLE BIND OFF

Step 1: Knit or e-wrap knit 2 pegs.

Step 2: Use the tool to remove the loop from the peg just worked and place it on the first peg, leaving the second peg empty ***(Fig. 7a)***. Lift the bottom loop over the top loop and off the peg ***(Fig. 7b)***. Move the loop from the first peg to the empty peg.

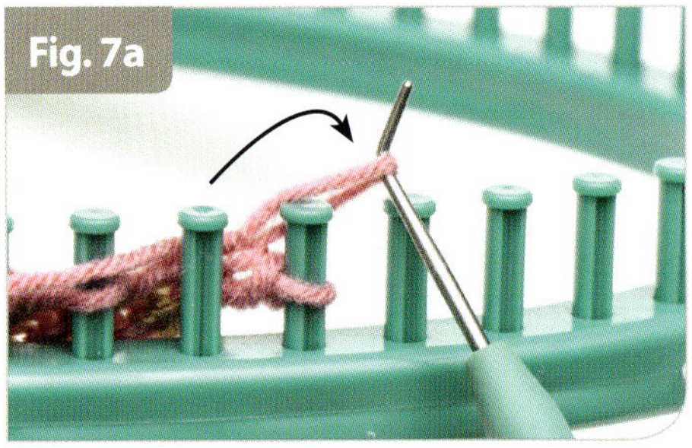
Fig. 7a

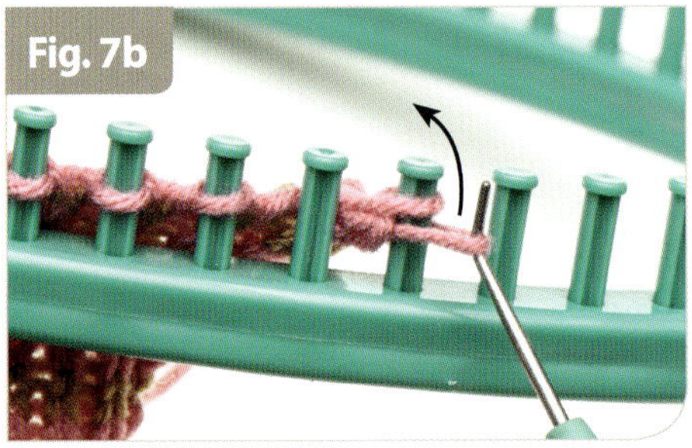
Fig. 7b

Step 3: Knit or e-wrap knit the next peg.

To bind off all pegs, repeat Steps 2 and 3 until 2 loops remain, then repeat Step 2 once **more**. Cut the yarn and pull the end through the final loop.

To bind off only some of the pegs, repeat Steps 2 and 3 until the specified number of pegs have been bound off.

DOUBLE WRAP BIND OFF

Step 1: Knit 1 peg.

Step 2: E-wrap next peg twice and knit it lifting the bottom loop over the top 2 loops and off the peg.

Step 3: Insert the tool in the top loop on the peg just worked and remove both loops making one long loop and place it on the first peg without tightening it ***(Fig. 8a)***, leaving the second peg empty. Lift the bottom loop over the top loop and off the peg ***(Fig. 8b)***.

Fig. 8a

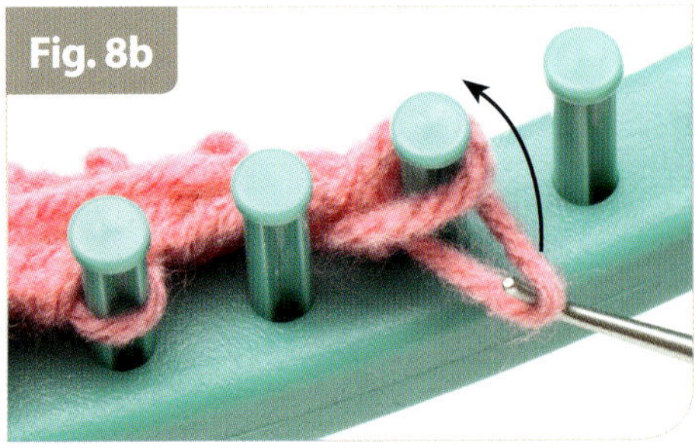
Fig. 8b

Step 4: Move the loop from the first peg to the second peg.

To bind off all pegs, repeat Steps 2-4 until 2 loops remain, then repeat Steps 2 and 3 once **more**. Cut the yarn and pull the end through the final loop.

CHAIN ONE BIND OFF

With the working yarn to the inside of the loom, insert a crochet hook in the loop on the last peg worked, from **bottom** to **top**, and lift it off the peg. To chain 1, lay the working yarn on top of the crochet hook and bring it through the loop on the hook *(Fig. 9a)*, insert the hook in the loop on the next peg, from **bottom** to **top**, lift it off the peg and pull it through the loop on the hook *(Fig. 9b)*.

Fig. 9a

Fig. 9b

★ Chain 1, insert the hook in the loop on the next peg, from **bottom** to **top**, lift it off the peg and pull it through the loop on the hook; repeat from ★ until all of the loops have been removed from the loom and there is one loop left on the crochet hook.

Cut the yarn and pull the end through the final loop *(Fig. 9c)*; tighten the loop.

Fig. 9c

Note: If the last row was worked from right to left, you will need to hold the loom with the inner edge facing while binding off.

SEWN BIND OFF

Wrap the working yarn around the entire loom 3 times and cut the yarn at that point, giving you a long enough length to work the bind off. Unwrap the loom and thread the yarn needle with the end.

Step 1: Bring the yarn needle down through the loop on the first peg, then down through the loop on the second peg *(Fig. 10a)*.

Fig. 10a

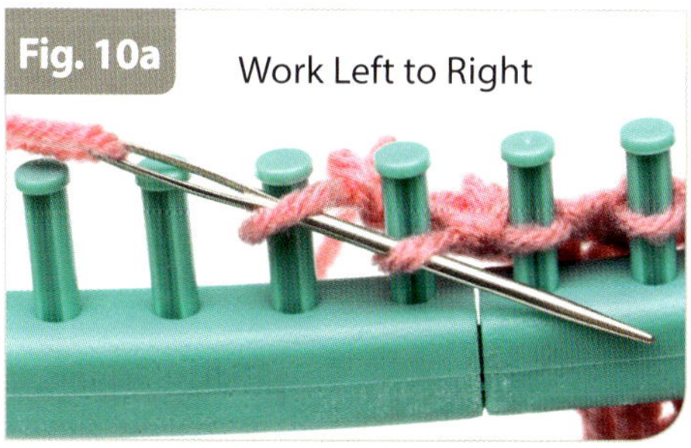

Step 2: Bring the yarn needle up through the loop on the first peg and lift it off the peg *(Fig. 10b)*, sliding it onto the yarn.

Fig. 10b

Repeat Steps 1 and 2 until one loop remains. Bring the yarn needle up through the loop on the remaining peg and lift it off the peg, pulling the yarn end through the loop.

WEAVING SEAMS

With the **right** side of both pieces facing you and edges even, sew through both sides once to secure the beginning of the seam. Insert the needle under the bar between the first and second stitches on the row and pull the yarn through *(Fig. 11)*. Insert the needle under the next bar on the second side. Repeat from side to side, being careful to match rows. If the edges are different lengths, it may be necessary to insert the needle under two bars at one edge.

Fig. 11

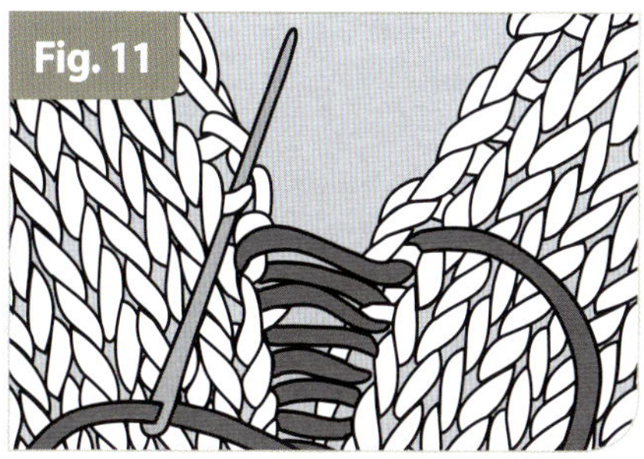

Yarn INFORMATION

The items in this book were made using either light or medium weight yarns. Any brand of the specified weight of yarn may be used. It is best to refer to the yardage/meters when determining how many skeins or balls to purchase. Remember, to arrive at the finished size, it is the GAUGE/TENSION that is important, not the brand of yarn.

For your convenience, listed below are the yarns used to create our photography models. Because yarn manufacturers make frequent changes in their product lines, you may sometimes find it necessary to use a substitute yarn or to search for the discontinued product at alternate suppliers (locally or online).

HEART BABY BIB

Lion Brand® Jamie®
#133 Peachy

GARTER BOOTIES

Caron® Simply Soft® Light™
#0005 Key Lime

LACY STRIPES BABY BLANKET

Lion Brand® Ice Cream®
#205 Spumoni

GARTER CHECKS COWL

Red Heart® With Love®
#1934 Autumn

CHECKS HAT

Lion Brand® Heartland® Tweed
Color A (Green) - #373 Everglades Tweed

Lion Brand® Heartland
Color B (Yellow) - #158 Yellowstone

BUTTON-UP GAUNTLETS

Lion Brand® Heartland® Tweed
#373 Everglades Tweed

LEISURE TIME PILLOW

Lion Brand® Wool-Ease®
#115 Blue Mist

LEISURE TIME LAP ROBE

Red Heart® Boutique™ Treasure™
#1930 Horizon

We have made every effort to ensure that these instructions are accurate and complete. We cannot, however, be responsible for human error, typographical mistakes, or variations in individual work.

Production Team: Instructional/Technical Writer - Cathy Hardy; Editorial Writer - Susan Frantz Wiles; Senior Graphic Artist - Lora Puls; Graphic Artists - Marcus Boyce and Leia Morshedi; Photo Stylist - Lori Wenger; and Photographer - Jason Masters.